BELIEVE IN THE
POSSIBILITY

Copyright © 2009 Sellers Publishing, Inc.
All rights reserved.

Cover and interior design by George Corsillo/Design Monsters
Cover and spine photo © Pascal Le Segretain/Getty Images, Inc.

Sellers Publishing, Inc.
161 John Roberts Road, South Portland, Maine 04106
For ordering information:
(800) 625-3386 Toll free
(207) 772-6814 Fax
Visit our Web site: www.sellerspublishing.com
E-mail: rsp@rsvp.com

ISBN: 13: 978-1-4162-0799-3

10 9 8 7 6 5 4 3 2 1

Printed and bound in China.

Credits: page 112

BELIEVE IN THE POSSIBILITY

The Words Of
MICHELLE OBAMA

SELLERS
PUBLISHING

"The one thing people are most curious about [is] they really want to know, how am I balancing this stuff? Balancing being a mother, a professional, a campaigner, a wife, a woman, right? . . . Like many women, I'm doing a whole lot of juggling. Juggling!"

"In my own life, in my own small way, I've tried to give back to this country that has given me so much. That's why I left a job at a law firm for a career in public service, working to empower young people to volunteer in their communities. Because I believe that each of us —

no matter what our age or background or walk of life — each of us has something to contribute to the life of this nation."

"Barack and I measure how well we are doing by saying, 'How are the girls?'"

"I come here as a mom whose girls are the heart of my heart and the center of my world — they're the first thing I think about when I wake up in the morning, and the last thing I think about when I go to bed at night."

"I loved getting As. I liked being smart. I loved being on time. I loved getting my work done. I thought being smart was cooler than anything in the world."

"The truth is there are millions of shining little lights just like me all over this country. Kids living in the shadows, being told by their own communities what they can and cannot do. This is an opportunity for all of us to send a different message to all those shining lights."

"All of us are driven by a simple belief that the world as it is just won't do — that we have an obligation to fight for the world as it should be."

"America should be a place where you can make it if you try."

"There's fun every day.
I have one of the best jobs
in the world."

"I know that right now I am living . . . in a very blessed situation, because I have what most families don't have . . . tons of support all around, not just my mother but staff and administration. I have a Chief of Staff and a personal assistant, and everyone needs that; that's what we need. Everyone should have a Chief of Staff and a set of personal assistants."

"Several things happened over the course of my life in a year to make me stop and actually think for the first time about what I wanted. I lost my father. I lost one of my good friends to cancer suddenly. She was in her twenties when she died . . . For the first time I had to think about life and the life that I was building for myself, and I had to ask myself whether, if I died tomorrow, would I want this to be my legacy, working in a corporate firm, working for big companies?

And when I asked myself the question, the resounding answer was, absolutely not. This isn't what I want to leave behind, this isn't why I went to Princeton and Harvard, this isn't why I was doing what I was doing. I thought I had more to give."

"I'm an information gatherer.

I want to talk to, and get . . .
many perspectives from
people, Republicans and
Democrats alike."

"We want our children — and all children in this nation — to know that the only limit to the height of your achievements is the reach of your dreams and your willingness to work for them."

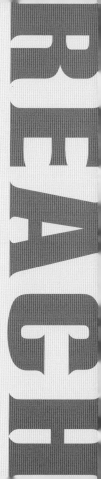

"I tell my girls this every day: It doesn't matter what grade you get, but it matters how well you do. And my question for them is, 'Did you do your very best?'"

"We have a real moment in history to once again come together to help our neighbors, our communities and to help our country."

"Women in particular need to keep an eye on their physical and mental health, because if we're scurrying to and from appointments and errands, we don't have a lot of time to take care of ourselves. We need to do a better job of putting ourselves higher on our own 'to do' list."

"There are few things more rewarding than watching young people recognize that they have the power to enrich not only their lives, but the lives of others as well."

"Being smart is really cool,
so get it together."

"There is no magic dust that leads to success. It is something simple: hard work, determination, and belief in one's self."

"I tell my kids, I want you to be comfortable with failing, because if you learn how to fail, then you're not afraid to do what? To try, right?"

"Solutions to our nation's most challenging social problems are not going to come from Washington alone. Real innovation often starts with individuals who apply themselves to solve a problem right in their own community. That's where the best ideas come from."

"The next chapter in history is written by you."

"I call myself a 120-percenter.

If I'm not doing any job at 120 percent, I think I'm failing."

"We want to use [the White House garden] as a point of education, to talk about health and how delicious it is to eat fresh food, and how you can take that food and make it part of a healthy diet. You know, the tomato that's from your garden tastes very different from one that isn't."

"Let's hear it for vegetables!
Let's hear it for fruits!"

"I love clothes. First and foremost, I wear what I love. That's what women have to focus on: what makes them happy and what makes them feel comfortable and beautiful. If I can have any impact, I want women to feel good about themselves and have fun with fashion."

"[Barack's] always asking: 'Is that new? I haven't seen that before.' It's like, Why don't you mind your own business? Solve world hunger. Get out of my closet."

"Exercise is really important to me — it's therapeutic. So if I'm ever feeling tense or stressed or like I'm about to have a meltdown, I'll put on my iPod and head to the gym or out on a bike ride along Lake Michigan with the girls."

"I'm still trying to find time for myself, getting the hair done — yeah . . . let's not pretend we don't know that getting the hair and nails done is important — and getting a workout."

"I really focus on what's in front of me at the time. And, really, when I go before a crowd, I'm thinking about trying to reach peoples' hearts."

"I feel the prayers.
I feel your encouragement."

TRANSFORM

"Meaningful change never happens from the top down but from the bottom up."

"You have to ask yourselves, what will you do in life to help someone else in need?"

"I tease my husband. He is incredibly smart, and he is very able to deal with a strong woman, which is one of the reasons why he can be President, because he can deal with me."

"Dream big, think broadly about your life, and please make giving back to your community a part of that vision."

"The one message that I have for all of you struggling with [the work-family balance], is just remember there is no right answer. It took me a long time to figure that out."

"National and community service
is near and dear to my heart.

It is the reason that I breathe."

"I know firsthand from [my parents'] lives — and mine — that the American Dream endures."

"I hope that Sojourner Truth would be proud to see me, a descendant of slaves, serving as the First Lady of the United States of America."

"During my college years I had to do work-study in order to get through. And what I had to do to get through, I typed, I worked at a bindery, I did a whole bunch of babysitting and piano tutoring and dog training. I did a little bit of everything."

"One of the lessons that I grew up with was to always stay true to yourself and never let what somebody else says distract you from your goals. And so when I hear about negative and false attacks, I really don't invest any energy in them, because I know who I am."

"I know that all I can do is be the best me that I can.

And live life with some gusto.
Giving back is a big part of that."

"Embedded in our nation's core values is a spirit of community, generosity and entrepreneurship. I saw all throughout this campaign in every corner of the country a can-do attitude that says that no challenge is too great for the people in this nation."

"Being the First Lady is like the icing on the cake of helping other people."

BALANCING

"Every woman that I know, regardless of race, education, income, background, political affiliation, is struggling to keep her head above water. We try to convince ourselves that somehow doing it all is a badge of honor, but for many of us it is a necessity and we have to be very careful not to lose ourselves in the process."

"As women . . . we've learned to . . . respect ourselves, first and foremost. And then we learned to respect each other as women, to treat each other with dignity and respect — not as competition, but with love and admiration . . . And then we learned to have respect for others as well."

"It doesn't take a lot to do something major."

"Let's roll up our sleeves
and get to work."

"I'm a good cook when I have time to do it, but I'm not somebody who has to cook. If there is somebody else who has got a good meal, we're there!"

"I love a good candy bar."

"**R**each back and find the person
behind you who you can help pull up . . .

Give them a boost, give them a pep talk, show them values — give them a clue on how to get where you are."

"Our future as an innovative country depends on ensuring that everyone has access to the arts and to cultural opportunity."

"Our common stories and struggles and values are what make this country great."

"It's important for you to be true to yourselves, not to worry too much about what other people are going to think or make of your choices."

"We try to set [Bo] up for success."

"I always believe that investing in the community that you live in . . . is critical."

"Home ownership, at least as I know it, growing up on the South Side of Chicago, has always been one of the building blocks for strong neighborhoods, for strong schools and strong families."

"Barack has been told in every race that he's ever run that he shouldn't do it, he couldn't raise the money, that his name was too funny, his background too exotic . . . but in every instance his view, our view, has been that if you tell people the truth you can connect with people right here and now. If you can break through the noise, then people recognize the truth."

"Never quit."

"The health and safety of our children is our top priority. This is what it is all about: the future."

"When one woman with a phone in her apartment starts a movement that motivates thousands, her cause can no longer be ignored.

When brave women challenge thousands of years of tradition and history and become leaders in their religious communities, they change minds.

When women fight to be educated . . . they change the future for generations to come."

"This is how real change occurs
— one determined woman
at a time."

"There are people all across the country, even in these times, who can lend a hand and volunteer at a soup kitchen, even if they don't have the resources to donate."

"I do know values. I do know what I believe in. I do know what makes sense. I know common sense, and I know when things are not right or fair."

"Never let setbacks or fear dictate the course of your life."

"When times get tough and fear sets in, think of those people who paved the way for you and those who are counting on you to pave the way for them."

DIGNITY

"Barack and I were raised with so many of the same values: that you work hard for what you want in life; that your word is your bond and you do what you say you're going to do; that you treat people with dignity and respect, even if you don't know them, and even if you don't agree with them."

"I am a working-class kid. I wear so many different hats in my life. The story I come out of is the story of most Americans' lives. The stuff we talked about around the table is the same. When you see your parents who don't have much getting out of bed and sucking it up every day, you learn a lot about values."

"You know, every time somebody told me, 'No, you can't do that,' I pushed past their doubts and I took my seat at the table."

"These soldiers, they get up every day and they hold themselves to these extremely high standards, the highest standards imaginable. They work hard to prepare every day, not knowing what tomorrow will bring.

Their dedication isn't just for their own sake, but for the sake of their unit and for the sake of this country."

"Military family members have their own special courage and strength."

COURAGE

DREAM

"I know that my daughters can dream big. They really can. There is no ceiling.

They can envision themselves any way that they want, surgeons, Supreme Court justices, basketball stars, they have images that I never had growing up."

"I never focus on what could go wrong — if we did that, we'd never get anywhere"

"I need stability and evenness, and not paying attention to media coverage helps."

"I . . . found my life enriched when I left my job at a corporate law firm. I thought that was the best thing I'd ever do, making a lot of money in a corporate firm in Chicago.

But it wasn't until I stepped away from the corporate track and worked in city government and eventually helped to found the Chicago chapter of Public Allies, an AmeriCorps program, a national service program, that I realized how important public service and community service was to my own development."

"What are the things that we can do differently here, the things that have never been done, the people who've never seen or experienced this White House?"

"Our job is simple:
Just be open, be honest, be real,
be clear, and have fun."

"Democracy . . . has room for lots of voices, which sometimes take us out of our comfort zones, but that's what makes it so meaningful."

"I know that each of us has a cause that we [are] committed to. So many of us are passionate, and working hard outside of our homes, and dedicating hours.

And I would like to find ways for us to support one another in our efforts, to think about ways that we can link arms within our states and our communities."

"The other day . . . [my daughter] was trying to ride her bike, and she was trying to get up the hill, and she was mad because she couldn't get up the hill. But the madder she got the harder it was for her to get up the hill, because she was spending all of her energy being mad and not focusing on getting up the hill.

So when she stopped getting mad and focused her energy on what she was trying to do, she was able to do it.

So sometimes if you spend all your time being frustrated about your bad day, sometimes it just makes it worse, right?"

"My children force me to keep my feet on the ground.

No matter what happens on any given day, I am Malia and Sasha's mom."

"People are decent and they're kind. They are willing to give you a chance to prove yourself to them."

"Perhaps Martin Luther King said it best. He said, 'Everybody can be great, because anybody can serve . . . you only need a heart full of grace and a soul generated by love.'"

"I saw kids like me who were using their loan money to help their parents pay the electric bill, and therefore they'd run out of money for books and couldn't feed themselves over the course of the semester . . .

So I just keep thinking about those kids who are missing opportunities by a hair, by a breath, by a parent, by a teacher, by a dollar amount, and I'm kind of working to make up some of that difference to the extent that I think I can."

"I'm doing what everybody does.
It's just that my juggling
is more public."

"I never consider myself
a finished project."

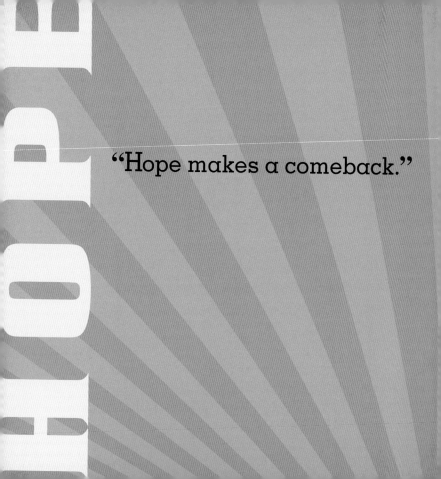

"Hope makes a comeback."

"We're all going to need one another in these times. We're going to need to keep lifting each other up in prayer and in hope."

Credits:

Remarks by the First Lady at Women for Obama Luncheon, April 16, 2007; Democratic National Committee (DNC) speech, August 25, 2008; Remarks by the First Lady at Women for Obama Luncheon, April 16, 2007; DNC speech; The (London) *Observer*, April 5, 2009; *Time*, January 24, 2008; DNC speech; DNC speech; *O Magazine*, April 2009; Remarks by the First Lady at a Corporate Voices for Working Families event, May 7, 2009; Remarks by the First Lady at a Corporation for National and Community Service event, May 12, 2009; *Newsweek*, November 5, 2008; DNC speech; Remarks by the First Lady on Take Your Children to Work Day, April 23, 2009; Remarks by the First Lady at Congressional Club Luncheon, April 30, 2009; *RealHealth* magazine, November 2007; Remarks of First Lady Michelle Obama at the "*Time* 100 Most Influential People Awards," May 5, 2009; Remarks by the First Lady to Employees at the United States Mission to the United Nations; Remarks by the First Lady at a Women's History Month event, March 19, 2009; Remarks by the First Lady at a Lamb School Hispanic Heritage event, May 4, 2009; University of California, Merced, Commencement Address, May 17, 2009; Remarks by the First Lady at a Sweet Honey in the Rock event, February 18, 2009; Remarks by the First Lady at a Corporate Voices for Working Families event, May 7, 2009; *O Magazine*, April 2009; "Washington Wire," *Wall Street Journal* blog, March 20, 2009; *Vogue*, March 2009; *New York Times*, March 20, 2009; *Marie Claire*, November, 2008; Remarks by the First Lady at Women for Obama Luncheon, April 16, 2007; *Larry King Live*, CNN, February 11, 2008; Remarks by the First Lady at Congressional Club Luncheon, April 30, 2009; Delivered at the DNC's Gay and Lesbian Leadership Council annual dinner on June 26, 2008; Remarks by the First Lady at a Sweet Honey in the Rock event, February 18, 2009; *Good Morning America*, ABC, May 22, 2007; University of California, Merced, Commencement Address, May 17, 2009; Remarks by the First Lady at Howard University, February 11, 2009; Remarks by the First Lady at a Corporation for National and Community Service event, May 12, 2009; 58: DNC speech; Remarks by the First Lady at the Sojourner Truth Bust Unveiling, April 28, 2009; Remarks by the First Lady at a Corporation for National and Community Service event, May 12, 2009; *Marie Claire*, November, 2008, *O Magazine*, April 2009; Remarks by the First Lady at Congressional Club Luncheon, April 30, 2009; Remarks by the First Lady at a Lamb School Hispanic Heritage event, May 4, 2009; Remarks by the First Lady at Women for Obama Luncheon, April 16, 2007; Remarks by the First Lady at a Women's History Month event, March 19, 2009; Remarks by the First Lady at a Capital Area Food Bank event, April 29, 2009; Remarks by the First Lady during a visit to the U.S. Office of Personnel Management, April 23, 2009; *Early Show*, CBS, October 17, 2008; *O Magazine*, April 2009; Remarks by the First Lady at a Women's History Month event, March 19, 2009; Remarks by the First Lady at the Ribbon-Cutting Ceremony for the Metropolitan Museum of Art American Wing, May 18, 2009; Delivered at the DNC's Gay and Lesbian Leadership Council annual dinner, June 26, 2008; Remarks by the First Lady at Howard University, February 11, 2009; *Time*, May 21, 2009; Remarks by the First Lady to the Department of Housing and Urban Development staff, February 4, 2009; Remarks by the First Lady to the Department of Housing and Urban Development staff, February 4, 2009; *Morning Joe*, MSNBC, November 13, 2007; Remarks by the First Lady at a Ferebee-Hope Elementary School event, May 13, 2009; Remarks by the First Lady to the U.S. Environmental Protection Agency, February 26, 2009; Remarks by the First Lady at the State Department Women of Courage Awards, March 11, 2009; Remarks by the First Lady at a Miriam's Kitchen event, March 5, 2009; *Morning Joe*, MSNBC, November 13, 2007; University of California, Merced, Commencement Address, May 17, 2009; University of California, Merced, Commencement Address, May 17, 2009; DNC speech; *Cleveland Plain Dealer*, August 2, 2008; *Time*, January 24, 2008; Remarks by the First Lady at the Fort Bragg Community Center, March 12, 2009; Remarks by the First Lady at the Fort Bragg Community Center, March 12, 2009; Remarks by the First Lady at the Women for Obama Luncheon, April 16, 2007; *Houston Chronicle* interview, February 28, 2008; *Cleveland Plain Dealer*, August 2, 2008; Remarks by the First Lady at the YouthBuild 30th Anniversary event, March 17, 2009; *Time*, May 21, 2009; Remarks by the First Lady during Greeting with Women of Excellence, March 19, 2009; Remarks by the First Lady at Poetry Jam, May 13, 2009; Remarks by the First Lady at Congressional Club Luncheon, April 30, 2009; Remarks by the First Lady at a Ferebee-Hope Elementary School event, May 13, 2009; *Cleveland Plain Dealer*, August 2, 2008; *Newsweek*, November 5, 2008; Remarks by the First Lady at the YouthBuild 30th Anniversary event, March 17, 2009; *Time*, May 21, 2009; *Houston Chronicle*, February 28, 2008; *O Magazine*, April 2009; *Larry King Live*, CNN, February 11, 2008; Remarks by the First Lady at a Miriam's Kitchen event, March 5, 2009